Keto I

The Complete Guide

Clarity, Simply and Easy Getting Started Guide for Lose Weight, Health and Fat Burn with Meal Plan and Low Carb Recipes for Ketogenic Diet in Busy People

The information in the following pages is broadly considered a truthful and accurate account of facts and as such, any inattention, use, or misuse of the information in question by the reader will render any resulting actions solely under their purview. There are no scenarios in which the publisher or the original author of this work can be in any fashion deemed liable for any hardship or damages that may befall them after undertaking information described herein.

Additionally, the information in the following pages is intended only for informational purposes and should thus be thought of as universal. As befitting its nature, it is presented without assurance regarding its prolonged validity or interim quality. Trademarks that are mentioned are done without written consent and can in no way be considered an endorsement from the trademark holder.

Table of Contents

Introduction

A good diet is extremely important not just to have a nice body, but most importantly, to be healthy. Often times, a healthy body translates to a healthy mind, and in this book, you will not only learn everything about the ketogenic diet, but you will also discover how it can have a positive impact on your lifestyle as well.

We understand how difficult it can be for people to lose fat and get back in shape, especially after stressful times and events. You are running around all day trying to provide for your family, and there is not too much time left to focus on good eating habits. Even though this is certainly true, it does not mean that you should give up on your health. There are a lot of methods that allow the everyday busy person to eat healthily and take care of their body, even if they do not have a lot of spare time.

This is why we decided to create this book. After helping thousands of people lose belly fat and gain a better lifestyle, we had to write down what we know, so that everyone can benefit from our knowledge. The ketogenic diet is a great tool to get in shape efficiently, while taking care of your body and without stressing out about dieting. It is a nutritional regiment that is easy to follow and that a lot of people, both men and women, have found beneficial.

Inside this book, we are going to reveal to you everything there is to know about the ketogenic diet, providing you with all the tools and strategies to make it work properly. The secret to losing weight is being able to keep it off when the "diet" ends. We do not believe in the concept of dieting and believe that the ketogenic diet can be a lifestyle. If you approach it with the same mindset, you can be sure you will have a lot of success and see results very fast!

There are hundreds of books on this topic, so thank you for choosing this one. Now let's dive into the topic and get healthier together!

Chapter 1: It Starts with Your Mind

"I'll start my diet on Monday!" How many times have we said this sentence or heard it. But that Monday for some people never comes or lasts a day. Here come the failures or the odious yo-yo effect, which often brings with it a lot of dissatisfaction in addition to the anti-aesthetic effect of stretch marks.

It's true that keeping the weight is not easy, especially when the finances and sources of income are so low that many people are having a hard time keeping up with their basic needs, even with their food. This is considering that while the vegetables are paid by weight, the so-called junk food offers bargain prices.

Another element that certainly does not make in favor of diets is the time factor. In a company that has always counted the minutes, you prefer a hypercaloric sandwich than ordering a healthy slice of steamed meat... and when you come back home late from work, the temptation of ready-made food is strong!

But it is equally true that diet is, first of all, a matter of the right mindset. If we enter the right mindset, there are no tight finances or tight deadlines.

Tell Me Why You Eat

First, we must ask ourselves how much and what we eat for hunger and for other reasons. Often, anger, sadness, insecurity, or boredom makes us open the fridge to unplug, at least for that period of time. It is the theory of compensation. It is the simplest, immediate, and most usable way to console yourself—often with sweet or otherwise high-calorie foods—from something in our life that we do not like or do not accept. This can result in more additional problems aside from psychological consequences because it can add more unnecessary weight, which can become your physical problem.

A short assessment of why we are swallowing food can help us understand what problem we need to solve or focus on what we would like to improve in our lives, and at the same time, block a sense of hunger that comes from the mind and not the stomach.

Psychological Tricks in the Kitchen

To give help to our willpower, we can put simple tricks into practice:

We know that the eye wants its part. And it is equally known that every taste is also involved in nutrition. We are not inclined to eat a dish with an unpleasant odor even if the taste is good. In the same way, a not well-presented dish sends negative messages to the brain. It is no coincidence that the chefs' skills are also a factor in the presentation of the dishes. The problem of portion reductions is often because of the lack of contents present in the dish. We must, therefore, circumvent the obstacle, such as putting out 80 grams of pasta in a smaller-sized dish instead of a regular-sized plate. This can trick us into thinking that we're already consuming a large amount of food when we're actually not.

"I can resist anything but temptation," said Oscar Wilde, which, when translated, means learning to make a reasoned expense. Avoid keeping snacks, chocolates, junk food, or anything that moves you away from the right path. At the same time, do not forget to buy healthy snacks, which can also easily be carried out or in the office, such as an apple.

Finally, realistic goals must be set. Thinking of doing lightning diets or losing an exaggerated number of pounds would be detrimental to health, and in many cases, often unattainable. This will only result in failures and frustrations, which can lead to giving up. It is best to follow the advice of the professionals and always set realistic steps so that motivation wouldn't be lost and you can keep continuing having proper nutrition.

Here are the five tips for adopting the right psychology to lose weight:

Recognize That You Can

Let's start by realizing that you can reach your ideal body unless you suffer from a disease that does not allow you to lose weight. Recognize that you can do it, that you have no real impediment to achieving the right weight. Look around and look for people in your same situation who maintained their weight or who have lost excess weight in a healthy and lasting way.

Impose Your Will to Your Stomach

Make yourself aware that it is the stomach that decides. The stomach chooses when it is hungry when it is full and not you. Listen and respect the signals that your body is giving you. How much time has passed since you heard your stomach make a strange noise due to hunger? If too much time has passed, rediscover it. How much time has passed since you got up from the table still with a sense of lightness and full of energy?

Be Positive

But not in the sense that you "hope" that everything goes well and you put bandages on your eyes when difficulties appear. I mean talk positively, encourage yourself, correct what you want, and erase what you no longer desire. Do not say what you do not want, but focus on what you desire to achieve. Talk to the present about what you want to be, do, and believe.

Do Not Listen to Your Mind

Think that the taste of something must always be associated with true hunger. If there is no real hunger, then the will to eat something tasty will wait patiently. Otherwise, you can satisfy your hunger with very small treats and enjoy them to the last one.

We all know that there are foods we are supposed to eat to be healthy and others that are better to stay away from. The news is constantly flooded by articles that tell us what we can and what we cannot consume. And if that is not enough, many of these messages sent to the population today are transmitted through media, the internet, and often by professionals in the food sector as well.

So, it is understandable to be lost in a world that, on one hand, does not lose a second to put under the nose and before the eyes, all kinds of desserts and, on the other hand, informs us about how they hurt and have a negative effect on our health.

A phrase that I often heard from people as a strategy to resist the temptations is the following:

> *"Remember, 10 seconds in the mouth and then 10 years in the belly."*

And so it is that in people, especially those who embark on a path of weight loss, conflicting feelings are created. On one side, there is the desire and the pleasure of consuming food such as a slice of chocolate cake, while, on the other, there is the sense of failure and guilt once the dessert has been eaten.

Prohibited Foods, Self-Control, and Guilt: The Recipe for Catastrophe

The desire for "forbidden" foods leads to the strain on our self-control by placing us in front of a "late-cost dilemma." Eating that cake today means I could enjoy the flavor and social context in which consumption takes place (immediate effect), but tomorrow, I will pay the consequences of my gesture with a little extra fat (delayed effect).

Even in public health circles, there is a strong conviction that to establish a certain degree of guilt towards unhealthy types of foods leads people to limit themselves in the consumption of those foods, pushing them towards healthier and better choices. This is a strategy that has been around for quite some time, and a lot of people have swayed towards it.

Unfortunately, the effects of guilt were not the desired ones.

In fact, we should consider that even the sense of guilt produces two different realities. The reality before doing the undesirable act of consuming is a positive sense of guilt that leads us to reflect on what we want to do and, that, therefore, could have positive implications in guiding our choices. The sense of guilt that is born and continues after having consumed our forbidden slice of chocolate cake is a negative sense of guilt that hardly ever leads to positive implications, and that is the more frequent of the two.

In most cases, the motivational reason we consume foods not provided by our nutritional plan is much stronger than the sense of guilt that is perceived beforehand. Therefore, guilt does not stop us from yielding to temptation. Often, we do not even have the time to implement rational corrective actions because the impulse to grab and put food in the mouth is too rapid. Once the consumption is completed, the sense of guilt is amplified, bringing with it self-criticism, loss of control, and loss of self-esteem.

A catastrophe-effect—driven by the sense of a lack of self-discipline—is triggered. For those people who are on a diet, the sense of guilt that follows a small cheat in the diet turns into a point of no return, a full loss of control without the possibility of remedy, and in your head, you hear that voice that says, "Great, now the damage is done, do whatever you want."

Some studies have compared groups of people who perceive "forbidden" foods as gratification/reward/celebration or as gimmicks/reasons for feeling guilty after observing how these feelings and perceptions about food affect their body weight and habit food.

It showed that the sense of guilt does not push people to have better eating habits and does not lead to better weight control over the short term or the long term. On the contrary, these subjects tend to maintain or increase their weight over time and have a tendency toward disordered eating that is pervaded by periods of restriction and binge eating. A further negative consequence of this guilt mentality is the increasingly low self-esteem they feel and the lack of confidence in their ability to improve as a person.

The people who, instead, perceive food that is usually considered "forbidden" as a food destined for moments of happiness and celebration have shown a greater awareness of food and make better choices in their usual diet. This perception has consequently led to a reduction in weight (if necessary) or to the maintenance of weight in both the short- and long-term. These people have better self-control as well because they are not driven by a compelling impulse, which is generated by food deprivation.

Freedom and Flexibility: The Recipe for Long-Term Weight Loss

To associate "cheat meals" with moments of happiness and celebration has been related to greater results and better maintenance over time.

According to Fredrickson's "broaden-and-build" theory, a positive state of mind is a resource that makes issues like "self-control problems" simpler to deal with. This goes back to positive thinking and the idea that we attract what we focus on. Have you ever had the feeling that everything goes wrong when you are in a bad mood? Well, the same goes for dieting. If you keep thinking and focusing on the fact that you are giving up your favorite food, it will be difficult to keep at it. On the other hand, by constantly reminding you why you are doing it and what is the goal you are trying to achieve, you will be in a much better position. It is not just philosophy, as you will see in the following pages. There have been many research studies on this topic.

Studies have shown that a positive attitude increases the ability to resist the temptation to eat "unhealthy foods." To conclude this discussion, a sense of guilt does not lead to positive adaptations. Giving people the knowledge about what they consume through programs, inputs, and campaigns on healthy eating does not lead to real improvement.

The pleasure of eating a good meal in a context of joy,

serenity, gratification, or celebration without experiencing a sense of guilt but rather with awareness, even if it is made up of "forbidden" foods, may lead to better management of your diet in the long term.

Therefore, it is appropriate to develop your mindset towards an easier, less rigid attitude. Some extra gratification inserted into your diet in a planned and conscious way will lead to better and longer-lasting results while reducing stress caused by excessive limitations.

Use Cheat Meals for Assured Success

We have understood that being too rigid in food choices and depriving ourselves of anything that could potentially alienate us from our physical fitness goal is not the best solution. What to do then?

Follow the advice of Oscar Wilde to the letter: "The only way to get rid of a temptation is to yield to it. Resist it, and your soul grows sick with longing..." Surely, resisting would only serve to get us away from our goals, so here is an alternate path to follow.

Plan one or more weekly "cheat" meals within your diet plan (the number will depend on the objective, the condition of your body, etc.) to gratify yourself and without any sense of guilt.

If, in the same week, there were more occasions, adjust the pre- and post-cheat-meals to minimize the effects of those extra calories.

And what do you do if there are unshakable reasons that make an entire box of cookies desirable? Rule number 1: Learn to stop before starting. Procrastinate and let the tide settle because stopping after biting the first cookie will be very, very difficult. Trust me, I have been there and have done it.

The first thing to understand is that when this happens,

there is something that does not work in the way of reacting to emotion or mood or in the management of the diet. Try to make yourself understand the real motive for that desire for food. Is it true hunger, a physical need, a desire, or a response to an emotional state?

Try to put your attention on the "usefulness" of that food as a serving at that time compared to a serving postponed for a few days until the planned free meal when you can give in to whims.

Consciously decide whether to consume it or not at that time and if, for any reason, your choice will be to consume it, make it clear that it is a necessary act without guilt (better half a pack of cookies today than a pack a day for the next few days).

And if all this had not been served and impulse had prevailed over reason, it is necessary to acknowledge what happened by clearing away any sense of guilt and weakness ("I am not able," "I am weak," etc.), reasoning about the triggering factors, and considering the feelings experienced before and during the breakdown so as to learn how to exploit them in a positive way.

This will serve to understand how to improve and, above all, start immediately on the right foot beginning with the next meal. An occasional episode of diet-lapse will certainly not ruin everything that has been done on other days when you have commitment and dedication.

Finally, when planning a diet, do not forget to include moments to "train the mind" as well.

If you follow a restricted-calorie diet, you know how difficult it is to be consistent with your food plan. Often, after having "sinned," we enter that tunnel of guilt and, from there, a vicious circle from which it is difficult to come out.

I know how difficult it is to be constant and to ignore all the temptations that call our attention, and especially our palate, every day.

I was there very often, too. So be quiet. Do not feel like a failure or one who fails to achieve his goals. We all have these periods. In those periods of high stress, it seems the only thing that can raise us is food. Sweet, salty, fried, or breaded.

You know, when I started to change my lifestyle years ago, I often deliberately looked for situations where I could test my willpower. I went to birthday parties (but I ate first at home). I participated willingly in the parties in the classroom, where the only healthy thing was the salad of the super-stuffed sandwiches the caring mothers brought. I went out with those friends that I knew for sure would never have a healthy diet.

Do not get me wrong. There were more than a few nights that I had to deal with resisting Nutella crepes, fries, and other things.

Surely, you're thinking, "But, were you crazy?" Well, yes, maybe I was a little.

But in a sense, I enjoyed resisting all this. Despite that my dinner was low in carbohydrates and high in protein and that it was usually around 8 or 8:30 at night, I was determined to be constant. Every time I came home after that kind of evening, I felt proud of myself!

Unfortunately, as they say, it was not always all sunshine and rainbows. Sometimes, I wanted to say that it was "too much." I sometimes ended up really believing (yes, unfortunately, it happened) that I'd let myself be tempted by the first junk food I saw.

I told myself, "just one, just to show that you are not fixed but that you only care about your health and your body." In the end, it went from one to two, then three, then four, to completely yielding to my temptation.

Those Were the Worst Days

I felt like a failure, one who cannot resist his mind. Surely, you will understand me. Not because I want to give you the failure! I would never allow myself, but because we all face these obstacles sooner or later.

We all find ourselves in these situations! Here are a few tips that can help you to get a better mindset.

1.

Tell Your Goals to Someone

When you have to be accountable to someone, things start to become much more serious.

Do you remember when, despite not wanting to, you did your homework? Then, you were accountable to someone (the teacher, your parents.) Even if doing homework was the most uncomfortable and tiresome thing in the world, you always ended with what was to be done.

It may seem absurd but accounting for something to someone allows you to have that consistency that otherwise you could hardly attain. When you need to do something just for yourself, take the matter very lightly because there is no one who could scold you or judge you. But when you are subjected to judgments by others, you are assured that, before doing something that should not be done, you will think about it and think again until you convince yourself that you really do not have to do it!

Whoever you want can be a good person to keep accountable to. Find someone who is really interested in you, like a parent, your boyfriend or girlfriend, and so on. The ideal would be to be accountable to a friend with whom you share this passion. We can better define it as your "Fit Buddy." Your Fit Buddy will be the person with whom you will undertake this path and with whom you will constantly be updating during your food day.

Establish a system of rewards and punishments with your fitness buddy, and each time one of you gives up, the other will have to give it a hard punishment. Be assured that this way, it will be easier to be constant, and you will hardly be tempted to fall into temptation. Whatever it is.

2. Do Not Buy Junk Food when You Shop

Keeping temptations away is the first step to avoid falling into them.

The supermarket is one of the places where we are tempted the most. Passing next to shelves full of sweets and unhealthy foods put a strain on our determination. Well, here you will have to arm yourself with all your strength and focus only on the foods that are part of your diet. Do not linger there to look at brioches, cookies, etc., and think, "I cannot eat them." Instead, think that by avoiding them, you will greatly improve your health.

If you are married and your husband does not follow diets and does not eat healthily, kindly ask him to hide all those foods that do not fit your diet, and that would distance you from achieving your goals. I believe that love is above all helping each other and what better situation than this to test his love for you.

If you really cannot ignore the temptations on the

shelves of supermarkets or still prefer to stay away, you can do your shopping online. We asked the owner of an e-commerce company to do a whole category for us. The category is called "Gym Sickness," and in it, you can find all the fitness products you need to achieve your goal.

We know how difficult it is to resist the supermarket and to stand up against it, we have also thought about this.

Create Healthy Habits

Good habits allow you to create the right conditions to progress in your goals and to be consistent in repeating them daily.

Replacing old and bad habits with new and healthy habits is not so simple. We have been used to unhealthy things for years and years. Our brain now performs them automatically, without wondering if it is right or wrong.

Some good habits could be:

- Waking up early in the morning;

- Going running;

- Reading at least one book a month;

- Drinking half a liter of water as soon as you wake up.

4. Read at Least One Motivational Book a Month

Keeping your motivation alive is essential! I have read so many books in my adolescence. I was neither a nerd nor the first of the class, but I loved to read everything I thought interesting, and that deserved my attention.

Despite the many books on healthy eating, those that really helped me achieve my goals were those on motivation! Reading all those success stories of people who have realized their dreams and goals gave me the charge to face up with all the difficulties that were on my way. All those beautiful motivational phrases helped me to plan the right mindset to become the person I wanted to be. I have read so many motivational and personal growth books. One thing is certain; this "category" will always remain my favorite.

5. Create a Positive Anchor Whenever You Resist Temptation

This is one of the techniques that fascinate me the most. The mind is something amazing and very powerful. Surely, you're wondering what these "positive anchors" are.

I want you to understand it for yourself. What is the anchor's job? To stay attached to the rock to allow the boat not to move, right? Okay, perfect. Imagine yourself as a great boat (not physically, of course). To remain stable, throw its anchors and grab a solid rock.

Whenever you say no to a temptation, whenever you can repel an invitation to dinner (knowing what will be waiting for you), whenever you go to the gym, whenever you have the strength to push yourself beyond your limits, whenever you are able to deal with a series of such things, you have to do something specific to remember to anchor that moment. It could be a gesture, eating food, a song, etc.

I'll give you an example: You're in front of the fridge, and you're opening it to get something you should not eat. Think back and close the fridge, thinking that your goal is much more important than any delicacy. Good. At that moment, for example, hold your breath for a few seconds and watch your hand while doing it.

On such occasions, repeat this gesture several times. After a while, your mind will associate the gesture of the temptation to a moment of glory, and, every time you are about to break, you will just shake your hand to bring out the determination of that moment.

These are all anchors and are used in neuro-linguistic programming (NLP). Although it may seem absurd, I assure you that they are very powerful techniques used above all by the greatest champions.

For example, try to think of the gestures that the

players do every time they score! Each of them has their own "move." That is their still positive. Using them will surely allow you to be consistent and focused.

6. Ask Yourself Why You Do It and Write the Answer on a Piece of Paper

Why are you doing it? I mean, why do you want to change your lifestyle? Why do you want to improve your body and your lifestyle?

If you do not have a real reason that pushes you to face all the various obstacles and sacrifices, you will leave at the first opportunity. But with this, I do not mean that if you do not have a super motivation, you will never reach your goals.

Motivation has to be really felt to be valid, and it can be anything you really want.

For example, you might be doing it for the following reasons:

- To be more beautiful;

- To please yourself more;

- As a child, they always took you around, but now, you want to show off who you are;

- You love to see the tone and beautiful linear bodies so much that you would like yours to be

37

the same.

Each of us has his own motivation! For example, mine was initially the desire to become an actor. I became interested in the world of fitness because I wanted to have a beautiful and perfect body, just like that of the actors. From there, I discovered the linear and muscular bodies at the right point of fitness models, and I fell in love with them. My focus has, therefore, shifted from wanting to have a dry body to wanting to have a toned and muscular body.

So, whatever your reason is, write it on a sheet of paper, hang it on the fridge, note it on your phone, do which one you want, but keep it in mind.

Trust me that you need to remember every day because doing all this will be a source of great motivation.

7. Have a Diary and Reflect Each Day on Your Journey

One of the most effective tools to create a habit is reflection. Having a diary in which to pen all our food intake is one of the best ways to reflect daily on what you really need to eat and what you did not need to eat. By doing so, you will be able to notice the obstacles that will arise along the way and decide how to overcome them. Knowing that you have to write in a diary about what you eat in a day is a great incentive to promise to keep a list of healthy and fit meals and foods. Writing a food diary is certainly one of the best habits you can acquire.

Losing weight is not always easy. It is not because overweight and obesity are the results of several factors that intersect, overlap, and intertwine. Nutrition and physical conformation are the results of elements such as genetic, environmental, family, behavioral, and lifestyle. What matters even more is that behind these elements, there are mental, emotional, educational, and cultural causes that lead to behaving in one way or another.

In a research published in the Cochrane Review, it was found that diet is not sufficient to lose weight in the long term. It seems that less than 20% of obese people are able to lose 5% of their body weight and not recover it in the next 5 years.

It seems that the most effective weight loss program, in the long run, is one that combines diet, exercise, and psychological support. Furthermore, increasing the duration of psychological support further improves patient outcomes.

Some Psychological Approaches to Weight Loss

Some psychological approaches have proved themselves useful for weight loss and maintenance of new bodyweight.

Cognitive-behavioral therapy was created by Judith Beck based on the planning of what to eat, carefully organizing the purchase, the creation of the environment, the planning of "moments at risk", reminding the goals of weight loss every day, and the management of thoughts that impede weight loss.

Mindfulness-Based Mindfulness Therapy (MB-EAT) was designed by Jean Kristeller of Indiana University, starting with the mindfulness-based stress reduction approach (MBSR) by Jon Kabat-Zinn and colleagues at Harvard University. It focuses on developing the innate wisdom about appetite and food. Mindfulness exercises teach people to turn their attention to the signs of the body, the hunger, the satiety, the taste, the consistency of what they want to eat. There is also an exposure phase in which people are faced with temptations. The focus is on satisfaction, the pleasure of eating more than on restriction. It seems this type of intervention is particularly effective in reducing emotional hunger and depression.

Biological and environmental factors. The factors that contribute to maintaining excess weight may differ from person to person. There is no magic recipe valid for everyone to lose weight. A study published in the Journal of Clinical Endocrinology and Metabolism found that leptin and ghrelin are able to identify obese people who are likely to reacquire weight after a diet. It is as if the brains of these people were more resistant to the stimuli of satiety. Other research has shown that people subject to emotional hunger, depression, or anxiety are more easily to regain the weight. Correlations between childhood abuse and obesity have also been found. Environmental factors such as poverty, lack of access to healthy foods, sports, lack of time, and other cultural practices play a role in weight loss and physical fitness.

Some Useful Strategies to Successfully Follow a Weight Loss Diet

Here, you can find some general tips that can be useful during your weight loss journey.

- Schedule an adequate amount of time each day to choose what to eat, buy it, cook it, and eat it.

- Keep a diary of the foods you eat, their amount, the changes in your body weight, the emotional and mental states related to meals.

- Divide long-term goals into sub-goals to be verified in progress.

- Draw lean ones after 6 or 12 months.

- Have realistic expectations, one that is long-term, to be reassessed over time.

- Think about all the activities that cannot be carried out because you're overweight and would like to practice once you have a leaner body.

- Do not perform activities simultaneously while eating.

- Avoid heated discussions in the family or work at the restaurant.

- Savor every single bite, trying to catch every little sensation.

- Take care of the appearance of food like the presentation, colors, the table, lighting, and all that can enhance your appetite.

- Chew for a long time before swallowing.

- Take breaks from time to time and enjoy your favorite food.

- Take time to just breathe and be with yourself.

- Pay attention to the mental and emotional states that are associated with food, choice, preparation, and consumption.

- Remove from the pantry, from drawers, etc. every unhealthy food

- Equip yourself with healthy snacks near you to avoid getting too hungry on the next meal.

- Always remember the goals of your weight loss and what drives us to do it.

- Do not dramatize in case of a snag, but consider it a possibility, but without becoming a systematic habit.

- Try to understand the reasons for the mischief and deal with it in another way that does not involve food.

- Celebrate your achievements in ways that do not contemplate food.

- Feed self-confidence, thank your motivation.

- Socialize with people who are experiencing a similar situation or who can still act as support and encouragement.

- If necessary, ask a professional who can support you emotionally for help.

- Construct their time in creative, rewarding, and fulfilling activities.

- Practice a sport you like, alone or in a group.

Eating is a necessary activity—the body is like a car, and without fuel, it cannot work. Unfortunately, in our society overloaded with food and obsessed with dieting, people build a relationship with extremely wrong foods, in which the act of eating becomes an automatic action and too often linked to negative emotions. In this chapter, I will try to explain to you the only thing you need to do to improve your relationship with food and make the act of eating an action that will bring not only nourishment, but also pleasure.

Have you ever eaten food without even knowing what they are?

Do not worry. Unfortunately, it happens to many people. Every day, people come to my studio to tell me how they respond unconsciously to their food stimuli, always repeating the same actions and, above all, feeling deprived of the strength to change.

They tell me how often they do not derive any joy from what they eat and, on the contrary, gain a lot of frustration or guilt from it, and they want to know what they can do to improve their relationship with food. They have often tried everything and feel tired and disappointed.

The solution is actually much simpler than what you may believe.

The only thing you need to do to improve your relationship with food is not to do stressful diets (which only lower self-esteem) or spend whole days in the gym, but something much simpler. You have to become more aware of what you are doing.

Increasing awareness of your automated models can help you make more deliberate food choices and improve your relationship with food.

What you have to change is not so much the food you eat, but more on your relationship with it. Learning to eat with awareness will allow you to understand what your body really needs, and it will allow you to enjoy your meals.

In this way, you will reach your ideal weight without having to constantly resort to exasperating diets.

How do you do it?

Simple. You have to learn to be in contact with *you*! You have to ask yourself some good questions to help you become aware of the hundreds of food decisions you make every day without even realizing it.

Here are some good questions you must ask yourself to become more aware and improve your relationship with food.

1. Why Do I Eat?

This is the main question that will guide all your future decisions. And in the vast majority of cases, you do not know why you're eating! People hardly stop to wonder what drives them to go to the kitchen and open the pantry drawer. Many times, one believes that they are hungry, but in reality, they only feel like that in response to an emotional stimulus, such as boredom or stress. Learning to recognize this difference is the first step to effectively fight your urges and discover the real needs of your body. Take a break to ask yourself, "Am I really hungry?" Whenever you feel like you need to eat, it will help you differentiate your physical hunger from environmental and emotional stimuli.

2. When Do I Eat?

If you have ever followed a diet in your life, you will have realized that the traditional dietary approaches do nothing but provide you with a food plan where they tell you what you should eat, how much you have to eat, and what time you have to eat! This cannot be more wrong. These rules do nothing but disconnect you from your natural nourishment needs and only encourage you to ignore internal signals of hunger and satiety.

3. What Do I Eat?

Diets are definitely frustrating. They force you to eliminate a lot of things, and often, the best ones in terms of taste! To be able to do this, you are required to have certain willpower that must be maintained for a very long time, which is very difficult even for the most persevering people. Learning to consume a little of everything in a moderate way, ranging from healthier foods to those that you eat for pleasure, will lead you to live your relationship with food in a much more balanced way. By freeing yourself from restrictions, you will develop the ability to respond to the wisdom of your body—that innate wisdom that is within each person.

4. How Do I Eat?

Quickly? Standing up? Watching TV? Many people eat this way and are so inclined to eat more—this feeling of satiety and satisfaction is, in fact, less when not paying attention to the food you introduce. Learn to avoid multitasking when you eat and dedicate quality time to the activity of eating. In this way, you will be able to feel what your body has to tell you, such as when it is time to stop, so as to avoid the binge you will later regret.

5. How Much Do You Eat?

Normally, classic diets focus on how much you are allowed to eat using methods based on the control of calories or fat. This behavior, however, in the long run, leads you to spend an enormous amount of time, energy, and willpower. Turning the meal into a mechanical experience will make you disconnect from internal signals, and this will favor problematic behaviors rather than reducing them. Paying attention to the signs of satiety and determining small goals in the situation, such as feeling better after eating than before you start, will make you able to eat the "right" amount of food based on the real needs of your body. For example, young children eat when they are hungry and stop when they are full. They touch, smell, and explore food while eating it. Re-learning these innate behaviors in humans is essential for developing a healthy relationship with food.

The idea of starting a diet can be daunting, especially if you are not mentally prepared to face such a change. When the mind is calm and prepared, sticking to a healthy food program is much simpler. With the right preparation, you will be able to effectively achieve your goals, and you will make it less difficult not to fall into temptation during the journey.

Be aware of the recurring negative thoughts related to food.

Oftentimes, our diets fail because of our beliefs related to food and eating. Try to become aware of your food beliefs and make an effort to change your mentality.

We often think that on special occasions, it is right to let go a bit. There's nothing wrong with eating a little more from time to time, but be honest with yourself about what you consider "special occasions." When events like eating away from home, business lunches, office parties, and other small events all become excuses to let yourself binge, the failure of the diet is just around the corner. Therefore, try to re-evaluate what occasions can be considered as "special" and when it is better to stick to your original diet plan.

Do You Use Food As a Reward?

Many think that after a long busy day, it is normal to deserve to go out for dinner or eat an entire tub of ice cream. Look for alternative ways to reward yourself, which do not include food. For example, take a long hot bath, buy a new dress, or go to the cinema. There are many ways to reward yourself without using food.

The Importance of Listening to your Body

Dissociate Food from Certain Activities

Food is closely linked to numerous social rituals. Giving up sugar and fat may not be easy when we emotionally associate them with certain habits. Make a conscious effort to break these dangerous patterns, as they can become a big obstacle to your weight loss journey. With this, there is a tendency to consume larger quantities of unhealthy food, especially during holidays. For instance, it is pretty common for people to indulge in cakes and pastries, even if they are on a diet, just because there is a particular occasion. How many times have we heard people saying that they will start their diet on January first? Hundreds, if not thousands. The reality is that there is no need to wait until a specific day to start a diet. The sooner you will start learning new and healthier habits, the sooner you will begin to see results.

With this, we are not saying you should not enjoy a piece of cake on your birthday or on special occasions. We are just pointing out the fact that associating "fun" and "happiness" with processed foods can be detrimental to your weight loss. Being "aware" of this trap is the first step to become healthier and, more importantly, to know when it is time to "let go" and indulge in what you like the most and when it is better to take a step back and realize what you are trying to do.

Try to be aware of the times you eat too much or make bad food choices, both in terms of food and the things you drink. Whenever you go to the cinema, do you buy Coca-Cola and popcorn? Cannot say "no" to a few glasses of wine during the evenings out? Cannot imagine a Saturday morning without coffee and donuts? If so, take the extra mile to commit to cutting these associations.

Try changing associations by replacing harmful foods with healthier ones. For example, when you spend the evening out, dedicate it to a board game instead of focusing on drinking. On Saturday mornings, have breakfast with coffee, yogurt, and fresh fruits. If, at the end of the day, you tend to try to relax through eating, replace the food with a good book or some music.

It Is Not Just about Calories

In the end, you will be more likely to be able to stick to your diet by committing yourself to change your negative behaviors rather than just keeping your calories under control. Try to become aware of when you eat and why you do it. Even if it is only half a biscuit, ask yourself if you are allowing it because you think you have had a bad day. Do you tend to eat because you are hungry or because you feel bored? If you do it out of boredom, try to get rid of this bad habit. Even if you do not exceed the calories you can consume in a day, always try to use common sense. Do not eat the wrong foods for the wrong reasons because it is the fastest way to associate pleasure with food, which is something you have to avoid at all costs if you want to lose weight successfully.

Ask for Help

Changing is not easy, and sometimes, we are not able to do it on our own. Ask for help from friends and family. Let them know you are trying to lose weight, and pray to support yourself. Make sure they know they do not have to invite you to parties where cheap food and alcohol will be served. Share your goals with all the people living under your own roof.

Establish Contained and Realistic Goals

Many people tend to sabotage their diet by placing the bar of expectations too high. Set achievable goals if you want to be able to stick to your plans.

Remember that a balanced diet allows you to lose about ½–1 kilo a week, no more. If you intend to lose weight faster than that, prepare to fail.

Initially, you should have cautious goals, so you will be more likely to be able to reach them and have the motivation to continue. Unspecific intentions such as "This week, I will eat vegetables every day," and something like, "The next time I eat out of the house, I will order a salad instead of potato chips" are valid starting points that can lead you to the road to success.

Keep a Diary of What You Eat

If you want your diet to be successful, you cannot exempt yourself from being responsible. Go out and buy a diary that will accompany you along the entire route. Record everything you eat every day and keep a calorie count. A tangible account will force you to notice your bad habits and motivate you to develop new ones.

Plan Your Meals

Planning meals and snacks in advance will help you not to give in to temptations. In the days before the start of the diet, make a list of healthy recipes that you intend to prepare. Try to get ahead, for example, by buying or cutting the necessary ingredients. If you want, you can also cook soups and vegetables to keep in the refrigerator—they will be very useful for the first week's lunches.

Focus on Concrete Behavior

When you limit yourself to making analyses in abstract terms, it will not be easy to develop greater willpower. Examining your concrete actions will help you start the transformation.

Make a list of the bad habits you want to change. Start with small, gradual changes. Try to commit yourself to abandon an old behavior for a week, and then continue making new changes slowly.

For example, you decide that after work, you will walk for 40 minutes rather than watching a show. Commit to respecting your purpose for a week. In the following days, you can gradually increase the duration of the exercise, e.g., by walking for an hour.

On the occasions when the willpower is not yet sufficient, commit to bringing yourself back to the right path, even if it may mean having to be particularly hard on yourself. Doing so will help you understand that you are the only one who has the power to change your behavior.

Recognize and admit your failures. Register them in your food diary. Take responsibility for your failure, learn from it, and grow stronger.

Describe the reasons that led to failure, highlighting your disappointment. For example, write something like, "At dinner, I ate dessert because I chose to, and I felt guilty after doing it." Although they may sound harsh words, many believe that saying them is useful to express clearly that they have failed. You will feel motivated to make greater efforts to be able to change.

For some, taking a weekly meal "out of the rules" can be a valid help to stay on track. A deprivation that has lasted too long may cause the whole project to go up in smoke. Sticking to a strict diet may seem more feasible when you know that at the end of the tunnel, you can give yourself the coveted food. If you think it might be useful to check you, consider scheduling a premium meal at the end of the week.

Three Meals a Day Is Not the Best Solution

Why do we eat what we eat? The simpler answer is that we choose to eat what we like. And it is a correct answer: satisfaction is the main factor influencing our food choices. But the question is more complex. Scientific literature has highlighted a link between food and the expression of both social and personal identity—we are what we eat, not only in biological terms but also in symbolic terms. In fact, food practices refer to different collective belonging and manifest individual adherence to a lifestyle. Moreover, social psychology, in explaining human behavior, takes into account the fact that we do not live in isolation but together with other people who inevitably influence us. Therefore, in addition to the tastes and information, we possess (for example, on the presumed healthiness of certain foods), the influence of others also contributes to determining our eating habits, often through the identification processes with different social groups. Without claiming to be exhaustive, let's look at some examples of social influence on eating behavior.

The first to influence us are certainly our parents, especially our mothers, who can condition us in different ways. First of all, through their example, our mothers are the first models we imitate in general and also with regard to the relationship with food. When we were in their womb, we began to taste and learn about the flavors of our family and our culture. This selective exposure to food continues throughout the period of breastfeeding (even our mothers' milk takes the taste of what they eat) and continues for a long time. In fact, at least until the children reach 11–12 years old, our parents decide which foods come into the pantry and arrive at the table. This type of influence is fundamental because the selection of the food we are experiencing greatly influences our tastes, which are mainly formed through simple exposure and repeated experience. They are built on familiarity—we like what we are used to eating.

A second way by which tastes develop is through associations that are established between certain food and a positive or negative situation. Parents can also influence these associations. If the family meal is a nice moment and an opportunity for sharing and living peacefully, our relationship with food will be connoted in a positive sense. If the meal is a battlefield, a place of conflict in which they force us to eat something that does not go well, then our relationship with food will perhaps be compromised and will haunt us even into adulthood.

Growing up, our peers become increasingly important both in general and as sources of influence on our eating behavior. Our peers influence us because we tend to imitate them. For example, at the end of a dinner with new friends, we often ask ourselves, "Should I get the dessert?" It may happen that we have a great desire for it, but if nobody takes it, we will probably give it up. Some research shows that people eat less if they are together with people who eat little and eat more if they are together with people who eat a lot. Why does this happen? In general, there are two fundamental reasons. On the one hand, if we do not know how to behave in a certain situation, which is perhaps new and unusual, we look at what others do to understand what is the appropriate behavior, and we repeat it. We also imitate others because we identify with them, and we want to feel accepted or at least not seem strange or deviant. This is where the idea of having 3 meals a day came from. As we will see in the next chapters, however, it is not the best solution.

As you can see, the importance of the mindset is very high, and it is safe to say that without the proper mindset, it is impossible to be successful with the ketogenic diet. This, however, opens the doors for something interesting. In fact, if we have the power within our own minds to be successful, it means that the outside world does not have an impact on our ability to be skinnier in the future. Most people that are currently overweight or that are trying to get back in shape oftentimes blame their circumstances or even other people for making up for their failure. However, now that we have understood the important role played by our mind during a weight loss phase, it is safe to say that we can take on full responsibility for our weight, and we can become the real master of our bodies. When you realize that you are in full control of what you eat and how many calories you consume in a day, you can decide what you are going to do about your situation. If you listen closely to the stories of the successful people that have lost an incredible number of pounds or kilos, you will see that each and every one of them started by realizing they were the only people to hold responsible for their situation. Yes, genetics and other factors can play a role, but if you truly want to achieve a result, you will be able to get the body of your dreams. This is an invitation to grow stronger and become a new person through weight loss and, to be more specific, through the adoption of a ketogenic lifestyle. If you decide to make a positive change, you can be sure that the people around you, those who really care about your health, will be more than happy to support you along your journey in becoming a better and fitter version of yourself.

Chapter 2: Basics of the Ketogenic Diet

Before getting into the details of the ketogenic diet, we would like to spend some time talking about the basics of nutrition. It is fundamental to understand the basic concepts before diving deeper into the topic. When we talk about diet and nutrition, we often do not know the principles that underlie our very existence and, above all, our physical well-being. We limit ourselves to eating something that others have advised us, and we often take advertised pills and tablets, which not only have no use but can even be harmful to our health and our finances.

In order not to get lost in the complicated world of nutrition, the first useful thing to do is an overview of food principles and daily human needs. This chapter will give you all the information you need to have a complete understanding of how your body works and how food can have a relevant impact on its efficiency.

Let's start by saying that all foods can be classified into five large food groups:

- Carbohydrates

- Proteins (or protides)

- Fats (or lipids)

- Vitamins

- Minerals

Carbohydrates are the nutrients most present in our diet. They are made up of two main elements—carbon and water—that, when joined together, give rise to the simplest of sugars, glucose. Aggregating them into larger molecules, they form two different groups of carbohydrates: simple sugars (consisting of a few molecules of glucose) and complex sugars (formed by long chains of glucose). A subsequent classification is that which divides them into monosaccharides (a sugar molecule), disaccharides (two molecules), and polysaccharides (more than two molecules). To be honest, things get much more complicated, but there is no need to be too scientific, especially if you just want to lose weight.

There are about 200 different types of carbohydrates, and often times, they take the name from the food in which they are in large quantities. For instance, there are some carbohydrates called fructose, lactose, maltose, but also sucrose and starch. Carbohydrates can be found mainly in vegetables, and their function is purely energetic and makes up the basis of human nutrition—providing about 4 calories per gram/weight. They are found in large quantities in pasta, rice, potatoes, fruit, milk, bread, flour, as well as in legumes.

They are the most famous nutrient since they are contained in so many foods.

The cells of our body transform all the carbohydrates introduced into the simplest form, glycogen, which, once oxidized into the cellular mitochondria, provides energy for rapid and clean use, i.e., without waste. These must, therefore, represent the basis of our nutrition and must provide about 60-65% of the energy needs.

However, it is rare to have to carry out a glucosidic supplementation. In fact, they are so widely present in all foods that perhaps we should think about reducing their consumption.

Fats, on the other hand, are complex acidic structures found in both animal and vegetable foods. Like carbohydrates, fats also have a purely energetic function with different caloric values. Lipids bring about 9 calories per gram/weight, and their burning rate is very slow. In fact, before being used, fats must be transformed into simpler elements, which the cell can then oxidize to obtain energy. In their complex form, on the other hand, they are easily stored as fat storage, which is the energy reserve of our body. Fats are often divided into saturated and unsaturated, depending on the type of chemical bond that forms the molecule. To simplify, we can say that saturated fats are "bad" and harmful to our arteries—these include cholesterol, glycerol, hydrogenated fats, fats contained in butter and margarine, palm oil, and most fats of animal origin.

The "good" fats instead are the unsaturated fats or

those contained in olive oils and in many seed oils, fish fats (omega 3 and omega 6), and lecithin (abundant in soybeans).

In addition to energy capacity, fats are involved in many organic activities, including hormone synthesis and cell membrane construction. Therefore, their function is vital, and our energy needs should be covered by lipids in the measure of 15–20%. This means that only 20% of the daily calories consumed should be fats, possibly good ones.

The integration of fats is very rare, as we usually tend to consume more than we should since they are the vehicle of taste and make us better appreciate the foods we ingest.

When it comes to proteins, it is a totally different story. They are composed of complex chains of amino acids joined together by peptide bonds. These amino acids can bind together in numbers, proportions, and different forms—giving rise to an almost infinite series of specific proteins.

There are 21 amino acids, 8 of which are called "essential" because our body is not able to synthesize them. In fact, human RNA possesses protein synthesis codes for only 13 amino acids and is able to process proteins that contain only these elements. For a complete protein range, it is necessary to take the remaining 8 amino acids, called essential, from the outside through eating.

Animal and vegetable proteins are made of the same amino acids—with a substantial difference. While each animal protein contains all 21 amino acids (in different proportions, depending on the protein itself), in the proteins coming from vegetables, there is always something missing. Some plant foods, therefore, contain certain amino acids but do not contain others. It becomes important, then, in the case of a vegetarian diet, to know how to combine the various products so that all the necessary elements are introduced. As we said, this does not apply to animal proteins, which are called "noble" because they are complete.

From an energetic point of view, protides are similar to carbohydrates, bringing about 4 calories per gram/weight. Unfortunately, the energy obtained from proteins is not as clean because nitrogen is released as a result of oxidation at the cellular level, which then evolves into free radicals, accelerating the cellular aging process.

The energetic process of proteins is just a fallback of the body in the event of an actual need for calories. Normally, protides are used for "plastic" purposes, i.e., they are used in the construction, repair, and renewal of all body structures such as muscles, bones, cells, organs, apparatuses, and tissues. It can be said that the human body is composed of 70% water and the rest of it is proteins. To maintain itself, the human body, therefore, needs a certain daily protein intake, which should be about one gram per kilogram of body weight (a man of 80 kilograms should take 80 grams of protein per day). However, this proportion can range between 0.70 grams per kilogram/weight (the minimum to remain healthy) up to a maximum of 1.5

grams per kilogram/weight. Beyond this threshold, there is the risk that the proteins you eat cause the development of many free radicals and other problems related to kidneys and liver. Ultimately, the daily caloric intake of proteins should be 15–20%.

The supplementation of proteins may be necessary in the case of a vegetarian diet (for the speech of amino acids), while it is almost never recommended in the case of a varied diet that also includes foods of animal origin. Moreover, the assimilation of protides for plastic use is about 4 grams per hour, so we can assume that the body has more means of using them for energy. However, the proteins taken through supplements are less similar than those taken through normal nutrition, as they are metabolized with a certain amount of carbohydrates and vitamins (especially B12).

Another important part of nutrition is the macro group of vitamins. They are organic compounds essential to life and development that normally the human body cannot synthesize, and therefore, must take with food. They are found in large quantities in vegetables, fruit, milk, and its derivatives. Many vitamins are sensitive to high temperatures, so it is advisable to take these foods raw. Moreover, some of them deteriorate over time and becoming bioavailable. This is why it is preferable to eat freshly picked fruits and vegetables., Each vitamin has a specific function, which can vary from the metabolic one (e.g., B12) to the one protecting the blood vessels (vitamin C). The deficiency of a certain vitamin, usually called avitaminosis, can cause specific diseases such as scurvy in the case of vitamin C deficiency. This is why it is important to have a balanced diet in terms of vitamin intake.

Vitamins are distinguished between two categories, namely water-soluble (which means they can be melted in water) and liposoluble (melted in fats). Our body is able to store the fat-soluble vitamins (A, D, E, K, and F), while it cannot retain the water-soluble vitamins (C, B1, B2, B5, B6, B12, H, PP) that are easily eliminated in the urine. The latter, in fact, should be taken several times throughout the day. It is also worthy to note that fat-soluble vitamins, which are stored in body fat, have a slower process of elimination. This can cause, in the case of high intake, a state of toxicity, thus creating very serious dysfunctions. Therefore, if the integration of water-soluble vitamins can be made lightly, we must instead pay maximum attention when it comes to the fat-soluble ones, which should be integrated only in case of established deficiency.

The last food group is one of the minerals and inorganic elements (i.e., without biological carbon) that cover multiple functions. They are often called mineral salts, but this is an improper name since most minerals are devoid of the salt part. Rather, they are single elements present in nature—metals, and non-metals—which use water as a vehicle to pass from the earth to the plants, and therefore, to the animals that feed on them.

They are divided into three groups, called macro-elements, micro-elements, and oligo-elements. This division is established on the basis of the daily requirement of the elements, which can vary from 100 milligrams/day for the macro-elements (calcium, phosphorus, potassium, etc.), to less than 200 micrograms/day for the oligo-elements (manganese, chromium, cobalt, etc.)

Although their presence in the body is around 5%/6% of the body weight, they are of vital importance, as they participate in many cellular and metabolic functions. For instance, just think about iron, which plays an important part in the cardiovascular system, or calcium, which is a fundamental element of bones and teeth. They must be eaten on a regular basis, as the body expels them through urine, feces, and sweat. A varied diet, in which vegetables, fruit, milk, meat, fish, eggs, and dried fruit are added, provides the optimal amount of all the necessary minerals.

Mineral deficiency, just like vitamins, can lead to specific diseases such as iron deficiency, anemia, or it can even aggravate diseases such as osteoporosis in the case of calcium deficiency. Therefore, a certain quantity of minerals is vital. But excess quantities can lead to poisoning. Hence, it would be good to stay away from the saline and mineral supplements unless there's an ascertained shortage. Most importantly, before starting the intake through supplements, it is advisable to seek medical advice.

After reading these pages, you now have a complete understanding of how nutrition works and how you can use the different elements to create a sustainable meal plan. In the ketogenic diet, all the calories will be assumed mainly from proteins and fats over a short period of time, but it is still crucial to have a balanced ratio of the different nutrients. At first, it all may seem complicated, but once you go through the rest of the book, you will have a much clearer picture of what to do to be successful with the ketogenic diet.

In the following pages, we are going to discuss what the ketogenic diet is and why it is becoming more and more popular these days. In fact, just by browsing the web for a few minutes, it is easy to find articles and blogs dedicated to this topic. Most people, however, decide to follow the diet without knowing what they are getting themselves into and are not able to distinguish good information from that which is harmful. This is why we decided to start the book by laying out the foundation of this diet, allowing everybody to understand its principles. Let's get started!

If there is a diet whose nature and modality are often misunderstood, it is the ketogenic diet. Exalted by some as a very effective means of weight loss, demonized by others for the supposed—and often exaggerated—risks that are ascribed to it, it is actually an important tool in a whole series of situations. It is a particular diet that must be used with due precautions and diligence, but which can guarantee relevant results where other methods often fail.

The premise upon which the ketogenic diet is based is the ability of our body to use lipid reserves with great effectiveness when the availability of carbohydrates is greatly reduced. The physiological mechanisms activated in this situation reduce the possible use of proteins for energy, protecting the lean mass, and significantly reducing the sensation of hunger.

In the clinical field, the first documented use of a ketogenic diet to treat specific diseases dates back to the 1920s when Doctor Wilder used it to control attacks in pediatric patients with epilepsy that was not treatable with the then available drugs. Its use returned again in the 1990s, and since then, it has spread more and more. In the 60s and 70s, with the constant increase of overweight and obese subjects, numerous studies were carried out on the use of a low-calorie diet that could lead to a rapid and significant weight reduction without affecting the lean mass.

The various protocols of PSMF (Protein Sparing Modified Fast) were born, diets characterized by a reduced protein intake with the almost total absence of carbohydrates, and a measured protein intake aimed at minimizing the loss of precious muscle mass. The spread of the ketogenic diet saw a surge with the appearance on the market of low-carb diets and do-it-yourself diets. One clear example of this is the Atkins diet, a model that drastically reduces the consumption of carbohydrates, allowing instead to eat fat freely and proteins. It is a grotesque caricature of the ketogenic diet based on improbable and fanciful interpretations of human physiology, rightly criticized by the entire scientific community.

In recent times, the emergence of the Paleo Diet has brought back into the diet food regimens the reduced carbohydrate content that can generate ketosis. Here, a solid scientific basis intertwines with perturbed, poorly-engineered biological concepts that have often generated grotesque solutions in which every carbohydrate is demonized and considered a poison, while the consumption of bacon is recommended, food which was notoriously abounded in the Paleolithic era.

In recent years, there has been a renewed interest by the scientific community toward the Paleo Diet, with the use of ketogenic choices for the treatment of obesity and for other diseases such as certain forms of tumors, some neurological diseases like Alzheimer's and Parkinson's, Diabetes, and the Metabolic Syndrome. The human organism has several forms of accumulation of reserves, of which the most consistent is represented by the adipose tissue. In an average individual weighing 70 kg, the total adipose tissue can amount to about 15 kg, while the carbohydrate portion amounts to less than half of a kilogram.

It is evident that the sugar reserves can guarantee energy for very limited periods of time, while fats represent a huge reserve of energy. Tissues receive energy in proportion to the actual availability of substrates in the blood. When glucose is present in sufficient quantities, then it appears to be the preferred energy source for most of the body tissues. When glucose is in short supply, most organs and tissues can use fatty acids as an energy source or can convert other substances into sugars, especially some amino acids such as alanine and glutamine, through a process called gluconeogenesis.

Some organs and tissues, such as the brain, the Central Nervous System, red blood cells, and type II muscle fibers, are not able to use free fatty acids, but under the conditions of glucose deficiency, can use ketone bodies. These are substances derived from lipidic parts, the concentration of which is usually very small under normal conditions but raises considerably in particular situations such as a prolonged fasting or a long period without carbohydrate introduction.

The increase in the concentration of ketone bodies in the blood resulting from fasting or severe reduction of their intake with the diet is a completely natural condition called ketosis, a mechanism evolved to cope with the stringent metabolic needs and limited availability of food of our hunter-gatherer's past, naturally also present in the morning after the nocturnal fasting or after intense and prolonged physical and muscular efforts.

The severe restriction of carbohydrate intake, through action on hormones such as insulin and glucagon, promotes the mobilization of lipids from the reserve tissues and their use for energy purposes. Given the scarcity of glucose, the present acetyl-CoA is used for the production of ketone bodies, substances such as acetone, acetoacetate, and β-hydroxybutyric acid, which become the preferred fuel for the cells of the Central Nervous System. During ketosis, blood sugar is maintained at normal levels thanks to the use of glucogenic amino acids and glycerol derived from the demolition of triglycerides to form glucose.

In physiological ketosis, the presence of ketone bodies in the blood passes from 0.1 mmol/dl to about 7 mmol/dl without determining significant alteration of the pH, which normally stays around 7.4. However, it may decrease slightly in the first days, given the acidity of ketone bodies, to return quickly to normal levels as long as the concentration of ketone bodies remains less than 10 mmol/dl.

The effect of saving protein reserves could occur through different mechanisms. The use of proteins is important in the first days of the diet, but as the body begins to predominantly use free fatty acids and ketones for their energy needs, the demand for glucose drops drastically, accompanied by the reduction of the use of amino acids for energy purposes. A direct effect of the ketone bodies on the protein metabolism and on the action of the thyroid is not excluded, with a reduction of T3.

The excess ketones that are not used at the level of the tissues are eliminated through breathing in the form of acetone, which results in bad breath, and through the urine, where excess acidity is buffered by simultaneous elimination of sodium, potassium, and magnesium.

Ketosis determines changes in the concentration of different hormones and nutrients, including ghrelin, amylin and leptin, and, of course, ketone bodies. It is probably through these variations that one of the most relevant effects of the ketogenic diet is determined. The reduction or total disappearance of the sensation of hunger that is typical in ketosis, undoubtedly, a situation that better help to endure the typical rigor of this diet.

The Science Behind the Ketogenic Diet

Do you like to follow a diet that would allow you to lose fat at maximum speed, and in the same span of time, allow you to maintain and gain new muscle mass? Well, I and some of my friends found a diet that does just that. We just followed a cyclic ketogenic diet. This is virtually a Sado-Maso diet, dedicated to those who embrace certain sufferings. But I can guarantee you that it works great.

To me, and to all those who followed this diet, it gave amazing results. It was one of the two diets experimented with the Ultimate America competition, and it really gave exceptional results even to those without a champion metabolism. But it requires grit. The basic principle is simple. The body uses the main source of energy available as fuel. Under normal conditions, the preferred fuel of the body comes from carbohydrates.

When you are on a diet, once the carbohydrates are gone, the body will convert part of the muscle protein into glucose (because the body requires it), which can result in the loss of muscle mass. If instead, you follow a rich protein diet, these will be largely converted into glucose by a process called glucogenesis and, once again, when the food proteins are consumed, the body will convert part of the muscle protein into glucose (because the body requires glucose, even in the face of the inevitable loss of muscle mass).

However, if there was a way to change the body's fuel, then the muscle proteins would be preserved. The ketogenic diet dramatically succeeds in this purpose. Fats become the main source of energy and, once the fat is consumed (since the body no longer requires energy as glucose but fat in the form of ketones), ketones will be converted into energy for the body.

After about 20 years of absence, the ketogenic diet has reappeared both in the slimming sector and in sports nutrition. In America (home from which food discoveries are born, both valid and useless), books like *Dr. Atkins New Diet Revolution*, *Protein Power* by Eades, and, albeit with less emphasis, *The Carbohydrate Addicts Diet* by Hellers, have brought back a low carbohydrate diet. Furthermore, in the sector of sports nutrition, two more but slightly different methods have come to public attention.

We are talking about *The Anabolic Diet* by Dr. Mauro Di Pasquale and *Bodyopus* created by Dan Duchaine. These two systems do not propose following a carbohydrate-free diet to the bitter end. Rather, they are based on a system that provides five days almost without carbohydrates alternating with two days of carbohydrate refill, a model used by athletes before a race.

Mauro di Pasquale and Dan Duchaine have written two

small books about it that I would define as "incomplete ideas." I have read them at least 10 times each, and from those bases, I started experimenting. Now, without false modesty, I can say that I think I am one of the absolute people who know the most. I have been on the ketogenic diet, alternately, for about three years. I studied books, articles, and anything I found on the web. Then I experimented with them. I performed ketogenic in all sauces and in all ways. For around six months, I measured my blood sugar five times a day until I got to the point of knowing automatically how much my glycemia increased with a meal and how much it would be lowered in how much time. In the next chapters, I will talk about how to put it into practice. I will talk about the target ketogenic diet and all the tricks to be applied to the ketogenic diet.

What Are Ketones?

The term ketosis, or acidosis, indicates a biological process linked to metabolism and nutrition.

In very simple terms, when the body goes down on glucose or on blood sugar, it tends to compensate for this lack of energy with increased production of free ketone bodies at the blood level. What are ketone bodies, and what does their concentration mean?

These are molecules of a lipid nature synthesized by the liver, but they have metabolic characteristics similar to those of sugars. This is why, under particular conditions, the brain stimulates greater production of free ketones. This concentration of ketogenic bodies produces acetone, which can be evident in having a bad. In fact, the brain's reaction is simply an emergency strategy.

When Are We at Risk of Going Into Ketosis?

The causes can be different. Some are pathological, while others are induced by the diet. Among those linked to morbid conditions, we surely find diabetes, pancreas or liver diseases, or alcoholism. However, recently, there is often talk of ketogenic diets, which cause acidosis in the body in a deliberate way, even if not for prolonged periods (because the health would be compromised otherwise). These are unbalanced and high-protein diets, in which the intake of carbohydrates (simple and complex) and sugars is totally absent. This should induce weight loss, and it is no coincidence that ketosis also occurs during periods of fasting.

In my opinion, this is a good solution, even if the diet is short-lived. Ketogenic bodies pass into the urine and through the kidneys. It is true that they may lead to dehydration, muscle fatigue, and cramps, but studies have shown that it is sufficient to drink a lot of water during the day to stay healthy. To restore normal metabolic conditions and regain strength, we must, therefore, reintroduce mineral salts and glucose into the diet or administer insulin if ketosis is induced by diabetes or pancreatic diseases.

The ketogenic index: Food can be classified as ketogenic or antiketogenic depending on its ability to convert to glucose in the blood. Foods that are primarily made of fats are the most ketogenic element because they can only be converted to 10% glucose. Proteins are in the middle because they can be converted into glucose with a capacity of 58%. Carbohydrates are converted into glucose with 100% efficacy and are naturally antiatherogenic.

The ketogenic index indicates how much a diet promotes ketosis and can be calculated with the following formula:

KR = (0.9 * F + 0.46 * P) / (1.0 * C + 0.1 * F + 0.58 * P)

F = indicates the total grams of fat supplied by the diet

P = indicates the total grams of proteins supplied by the diet

C = indicates the total grams of carbohydrates provided by the diet

A ketogenic index equal to or greater than 1.5 promotes a rapid establishment of the state of ketosis.

What Exactly Does It Mean to be in a Ketosis State?

Ketosis simply indicates a metabolic state in which the concentration of ketone bodies in the blood is greater than the concentration of glucose. However, this is not to be compared to the ketoacid state that occurs in diabetic subjects.

Being in ketosis involves two things:

1. The power of the metabolism of fats has been activated.

2. The entire fat degradation system is in perfect condition and is efficient.

Usually, the state of ketosis is a source of concern for doctors. However, unless you are in serious medical conditions like diabetes, excess ketones are easily pushed out the body through the urine. This permits a person to control the intensity of ketosis, which can e monitored using Ketosticks.

The ideal time to measure your ketosis level is in the morning, as during the day, the ketones could be used entirely for energy purposes, and therefore, may not be detected by the Ketostick.

Effects on the Metabolism of the Ketogenic Diet

The creation of a ketosis state, even for small periods of time, increases the body's ability to use fat as fuel. Furthermore, glucose oxidation decreases as the ketone bodies provide most of the energy the organism needs. In addition, a ketogenic diet improves the ability to oxidize fats even in well-trained athletes.

One argument for discussion is whether the ketogenic diet favors or not saving the body proteins compared to a diet of equal calories but high in carbohydrates. Several studies seem to try saving protein. Other reliable data from observations seem to support the idea that the ketogenic diet prevents proteins from being used as an energy source.

Since there is an almost unlimited source of fats in the body that can convert into ketones, and since they can be oxidized by every tissue, there is no request for the body to convert proteins into glucose by glucogenesis. However, it is appropriate for a normal person to take at least 1 gram of protein x kilogram of body weight. While for an athlete, 2.2 grams x kg of body weight is ideal. It is good not to exceed 2.5 grams because, as already mentioned, some amino acids are converted into glucose, causing an insulin reaction.

Other Effects of Low Carbohydrates Diets

It has been proven that an almost carbohydrate-free diet will allow greater lipolysis and a greater release of glycerol compared to a normal or high carbohydrate diet. This is due to the total lack of insulin, which blocks lipolysis even at small concentrations, and the fact that the production of GH (growth hormone) is increased, which also has a lipolytic action and also increases glucagon, catecholamines, and glucocorticoids.

The increase in the amount of growth hormone, due to the ketogenic diet, not only promotes lipolysis but also prevents the inevitable loss of protein that would instead occur with a normal low-calorie diet.

I hope you now understand what happens when a condition of ketosis is established through the abolition of carbohydrates and an appropriate ratio between fats and proteins, and training. All this suggests that the reduction of insulin, combined with the new hormonal condition, maximizes the oxidation of fats. However, some lucky individuals are able to obtain excellent results without reaching such extreme diets. It is also possible to improve the hormonal pattern through some small tricks.

For example, decreasing the number of carbohydrates consumed and making use of foods with a low glycemic index in place of carbohydrates with a high glycemic index will lower the level of insulin. It can also help to ingest foods rich in fiber. You can also never eat carbohydrates alone but combine them with fats and proteins (such as the 40/30/30 diet). This favors a more gradual release of blood glucose and a balance between insulin and glucagon.

So far, we have discussed what the ketogenic diet is. But what interests the athletes is not so much a continuous keto regimen but more of a cyclic keto regimen. What is this? It is a diet that consists of a period of total deprivation of carbohydrates with only a few days where you do a refill of carbohydrates. In fact, the issue with every diet is the consequential loss of muscle tissue.

Loss of muscles is also a cause of slowed metabolism. Although the ketogenic diet is the most effective way to prevent the loss of contractile proteins (muscles), it is possible that some muscle tissue is lost just the same if you continue this type of diet indefinitely. This is why two days high in calories and rich in carbohydrates fill the reservoirs of glycogen muscles (for training in the next week) again and stimulate anabolism and promote muscle growth.

What science still cannot explain is why the two days of high carbohydrates do not modify the metabolic adaptations stimulated by ketosis. It would seem possible because it takes several days to induce a state of ketosis, so it takes some time before the body gets used to the normal carbohydrate metabolism. This is an area that still needs specific research.

The Refilling of Carbohydrates

Usually, with a normal diet, muscle glycogen stores are always full. Under normal circumstances, an average person has about 350 grams. The consumption of these carbohydrates through diet and training followed by intake of many carbohydrates can duplicate this amount. During a normal diet, training has the ability to push up insulin sensitivity of the body, which pushes up a muscle's capability to get insulin in the receptors. However, this push up in insulin sensitivity happens only in a well-trained body. This push up in sensitivity seems to occur as a result of glycogen consumption in the stronger muscles. Moreover, following a low carb regiment promotes the activity of the enzymes responsible for the accumulation of glycogen in the muscles.

So, if we put all the pieces together, we see that a carbohydrate-free diet, combined with a workout that runs out of glycogen stores, followed by a high carbohydrate diet promotes super-compensation of glycogen. It must also be said that a complete super-compensation of the muscles can take 3 or 4 days, even if most of the glycogen is stored in the first 24 hours. It can be said that the muscles are able to store 9 grams up to a maximum of 16 grams of carbohydrates per kg of lean mass.

For every gram of carbohydrates stored in the muscles, if you drink enough, another 4 grams of water will be retained in the muscles. As already mentioned, an average person (65 kg of lean mass) who follows a normal diet will have about 350 g of glycogen in the muscles. Since every gram of sugar holds 4 grams of water, it follows that it will also have 1 liter of water kept in the cells. With a super-compensation at 12 grams, it is possible, in theory, to store 1040 g of carbohydrates, which in turn, will retain 4160 g of water. This is an increase of about 3 times. Recent research shows that protein anabolism is also stimulated by the degree of cellular hydration. So, this super-compensation would send an anabolic signal to the cells.

Are There Any Side Effects?

The main one is fatigue, especially during the first week. One study even showed a decline in mental performance during the first week. However, this disappears as the diet is followed.

One of the most frequently asked questions is what effect this diet will have on the lipid profile of the blood. As you follow a low-calorie regimen, all ingested fats will be used as energy, and in addition to that, body fat will also be consumed. Healthy people will find an improvement in cholesterol values. Like any diet that causes drastic changes, it would be appropriate to do a blood test before starting and one after a few weeks.

Since it is a diet that almost completely eliminates carbohydrates, it also causes nutritional deficiencies. Therefore, it is essential that people who undergo this diet must take a good multivitamin and multimineral supplement. In addition, it is also essential to take a good fiber supplement.

Since the diet is high in fats, there is a greater production of free radicals, and therefore, it is not bad to make use of antioxidant supplements as well.

Who Should Not Follow the Ketogenic Diet?

The ketogenic diet is certainly excellent for increasing your health and energy level. Nonetheless, not everyone can follow this diet. If you fall within one of these categories that I am about to mention, I recommend that you do not follow the ketogenic diet for safety reasons.

Pregnant Women

In this state, the body needs nutrients that derive from different sources. So, drastically restricting the sources of starches may have a negative impact on your child's health.

Women Who Are Breastfeeding

During this stage, women need oxaloacetate, an essential compound to create lactose for breast milk, which is essential for the baby's growth.

Athletes Ready to Begin a New Season

Athletes could get huge benefits from producing energy through ketones, but it can take 4 to 6 weeks before your body reaches ketosis. During this time, since your body has not yet gotten used to consuming fats as a source of energy, this can prevent you from achieving your optimal performance. To get the most out of a keto diet, give your body the time to adapt itself.

People Who Have Had Their Gallbladder Removed

Your gallbladder has the task of storing waste, giving your digestive system the ability to absorb the fat sources in the appropriate manner. Without the gallbladder, the fat sources are not absorbed in the right way. This can lead to nutritional deficiency. Why does this happen? It happens because most of the calories in this type of food come from fats.

People Who Have Had Kidney Problems

If you have kidney issues in the past, the ketogenic diet could push up your chances of having kidney stones again. This is because the ketones increase the production of uric acid. On the other hand, if you have never had them, kidney stones can be prevented with a ketogenic diet because it increases the consumption of potassium thanks to the vegetables. Keeping yourself hydrated during the day helps decrease your chances of getting them again.

People Still in Their Growing Phase

This is because the ketogenic diet reduces the production of an essential hormone in the development of the bones and muscles of children and young adults.

Try typing "ketogenic diet" in a Google search. You will find more than 500,000 results linked to many sites, which are more or less reliable, and which explain how useful the diet is when used to lose weight quickly. Do you know the secret of the diet? The ketogenic diet eliminates sugars and carbohydrates.

There are those who propose the "paleo" version, inspired by the diet of primitive men. But is the ketogenic diet really so simple and affordable for everyone? Not exactly. To clarify is a document prepared by the experts of the American Association of Dietetics and Clinical Nutrition (ADI), based on the review of the most recent clinical studies conducted on the subject.

The ketogenic diet is based on the reduction or complete elimination of sugars from food for a short period of time. In search of alternative sources of energy, the body begins to burn fat, processing in the liver the substances called "ketone bodies" such as beta-hydroxybutyrate, acetoacetic acid, and acetone.

Acetone is a transient metabolic disorder that in children can be caused by a feverish episode or prolonged fasting, an example of a "natural" ketogenic diet.

The production of ketones is indeed a sort of emergency plan, which serves to supply new fuel to the brain when it finishes the reserves of glucose.

The ketogenic diet can be considered as a medicine, and therefore, should not be done alone at home without the supervision of a doctor. Because of its physiological action at the central nervous system, it is recommended in cases of drug-resistant epilepsy. Some specialists also suggest it for the treatment of the most severe headaches, while new studies are evaluating its possible application in the field of neurodegenerative diseases like Parkinson's and Alzheimer's.

The ADI experts also remember its use in severe cases of obesity or refractory obesity, for example, in patients who must quickly lose weight to undergo surgery or to prepare for bariatric surgery. Moderate ketosis can also offer benefits in the case of type 2 diabetes, metabolic syndrome, and fatty liver (non-alcoholic fatty liver disease, NAFLD).

The ketogenic diet is contraindicated in pregnant and lactating women, in people suffering from hepatic, cardiac, or renal insufficiency, in young people with type 1 diabetes, in subjects with mental and behavioral disorders (anorexia, alcohol, and drug abuse), and in those who suffer from unstable angina, arrhythmias, porphyria, or have recently had a heart attack.

The ketogenic diet requires well-established goals and deadlines right from the start. It is usually carried out in cycles of three or four weeks, although some clinical trials have gone up to 12 weeks as well. The desirable weight loss is about 1-2 kilos a week, with peaks of up to 2.5 kilograms at the beginning. Please keep in mind that the scope of every diet should be to become healthier, not necessarily lose weight.

The diet should be modulated and customized according to the needs of the individual patient. In general, 30 to 50 grams of carbohydrates per day can be taken (less than 1 gram per pound of reasonable body weight), reaching the maximum level in males and large-sized individuals. The recommended protein intake is about 1 gram per pound of body weight per day, and the lipid level between 15 and 30 grams per day. The total kilocalories must be from 600 to 800 per day (to which are added to the kilocalories produced by the synthesis of ketone bodies, which are high in energy content).

If you use natural foods or whole foods, the diet may be a bit "limited and repetitive." For this reason, there are meals and substitute foods prepared only for particular occasions. ADI experts recommend a gradual diet, starting from more markedly hypocaloric and high protein, modifying in the next steps the protein intake (gradually reducing them) and the calories (to be increased just as gradually), with 3 to 4 phases each lasting an average of two weeks.

What Problems Can You Have?

Headache is the most frequent early side effect. Present in about a third of patients, it tends to disappear spontaneously within 72 hours. Subsequently, halitosis has been reported in the past (many patients report the need to use oral sprays or chewing gum, strictly without sources of carbohydrates), xerostomia (dry mouth), and constipation. Some patients also complain of reduced cold tolerance and postural vertigo.

For some time, there has been a total inversion with regard to the principles of weight loss and the basics of muscular anabolism.

Classic Approach

Food-induced Thermogenesis

The fundamentals of "traditional" dietetics suggest losing weight by also exploiting the specific dynamic action of food (ADS), or energy expenditure attributed to digestive, absorption, and metabolic processes.
In practice, with the same calories introduced in increasing the division of meals, it is possible to burn more energy to process them. This allows you to reduce the amount of time "on an empty stomach," avoiding the "hunger" and keeping the metabolism speedy.

Cortisol and Thyroid Hormones

Some argue that this practice also favors the containment of an unwanted hormone, cortisol (also called "stress hormone") and maintenance of thyroid function (TSH and T3). Obviously, this system works as long as the caloric amount, the nutritional distribution, and the glycemic load-gauges of the meals are appropriate.

Preventing Catabolism

At the same time, in the context of muscle growth, it is (or was) a common opinion that to promote anabolism, it was necessary to "feed" continuously (and "as much as possible," avoiding the increase of fat) muscle fiber cells in order to cancel any form of catabolism and promote photosynthesis, especially thanks to the insulin stimulus.

CPSIA information can be obtained
at www.ICGtesting.com
Printed in the USA
BVHW041403050521
606516BV00014B/454